Learn French for Adult Beginners

Speak French in 30 Days and Learn Everyday Words and Phrases

GW00645088

Table of Contents

Free Audiobook

French Fundamentals To Start Conversing Quickly!

SCAN TO ACCESS

Scan QR code above to claim your free audiobook!

— OR —

visit exploretowin.com/frenchaudio30

Introduction

Bonjour et bienvenue dans mon livre sur l'apprentissage du français!

I don't expect you to understand a word of that right now but, by the end, you will! All that French phrase says is, *"Hello, and welcome to my book on learning French!"*

If you have never been to France, you are missing out on a treat. It's a beautiful country, packed with iconic landmarks, beautiful beaches, stunning ski resorts, top-class architecture and art, some of the most beautiful countryside found anywhere in Europe, and, of course, we can't forget the food, wine, and people!

So, why are you reading this book? Perhaps you've decided to spend your next holiday in France, or you may have been offered a job there. Or perhaps you just want to learn a new language. Well, congratulations on choosing French. It's a wonderful language to learn, and even though many French people speak perfect English, I can tell you from my experiences living abroad, the locals love it when you try to speak their language. And the more you try, the more they will help you!

What will I be teaching you? Well, it's not a long book, so I've tried to cram a little bit of everything in to give you a sound basis in the language. Over four chapters, I've covered some of the most basic subjects you need to learn and have included grammar and real-life scenarios for you to practice. Each chapter also includes a set of exercises to help you utilize what you learned. You will find pronunciation guides and full French to English translations, everything you need to learn basic French.

Bonne chance et amusez-vous bien! (Good luck and have fun!)

Chapter 1: Salut Mes Amis! (Hello My Friends!)

In the French language, there are two types of situations: Formal and Informal. Informal situations are generally between friends or someone known. In contrast, Formal situations are at the workplace with your boss or maybe at a restaurant with a stranger. The vocabulary is different for Formal and Informal situations. There are some words that can be used only in Formal situations, some words that can be used in Informal situations, and some that can be used in both Formal and Informal situations.

In this chapter, we'll focus on Informal situations.

Let us begin by learning some basic vocabulary words.

Vocabulary Words

Word	Meaning	Pronunciation
Salut	Hello	S – eh – l – u
Coucou	Hello	K – oo – k – oo
Tchao	Bye	Ch – aa – o
Au revoir	Bye	O – r – uh – wa - r
S'il te plait	Please	S – i – l – t – p – l - ay
De rien	You're welcome	D – ri – ah
Je t'en prie	Please	J – t – o – p – r – i
Tiens	Here it is / Hold it	Ti – ah
Dis-moi	Tell me	Di – m – wa
Excuse-moi	Excuse me	X – k – u – z – ay – m – wa
Crois-moi	Believe me	K – r – wa – m – wa
Arrête	Stop	A – r – eh – t
Ça va ?	Fine?	Sa – va

Verbs

There are two main categories of verbs in French: Regular and Irregular Verbs (Verbes réguliers et irréguliers)

The verbs that end with "er" are regular verbs. For example: Regarder (To watch), Danser (To dance), Parler (To speak), etc.

Verbs that do not end with" er" are irregular verbs. For example: Boire (To drink), Devoir (Must / Have to)

Before learning the conjugations, let us see the subjects:

Word	Meaning /Explanation	Pronunciation
Je	I	J
Tu	You (Informal) / It is used to refer to one person	T – u
Vous	You (Formal) / It can be used to refer to one or more persons	V – oo
Il	He	I – l
Elle	She	Eh – l
Nous	We (Formal)	N – oo
On	We (Informal) / One (Example: One should drink water, here we replace one with "on")	O
Ils	They (It is used to refer to a group of people. This group can be of all males or a mix of males and females)	I – l

Elles	They (It is used to refer to a group of people. This group has to be all females)	Eh – l

Regular Verbes (Verbes Réguliers)

Conjugation Rule: Replace the "er" from the root verb with the following endings:

Je – e
Tu – es
Il / Elle / On – e
Nous – ons
Vous – ez
Ils / Elles - ont

Let us see some examples:

Verb	Meaning	Pronunciation
Aimer	To like	Ay – may
J'aime	I like / I am liking	J – eh – m
tu aimes	You like / You are liking	T – u – eh – m
il/elle/on aime	He / She / We like / He / She is liking / We are liking	Il eh – m / eh – l eh – m / o n - eh – m
vous aimez	You like / You are liking	V – oo z eh – may
Nous aimons	We like / We are liking	N – oo z eh - mo
Ils/Elles aiment	They like / They are liking	Il z eh – m / eh – l z eh – m

4

Verb	Meaning	Pronunciation
Skier	To ski	S – ki – ay
Je skie	I ski / I am skiing	J
Tu skies	You ski / You are skiing	T – u
Il/Elle / On skie	He / She / We ski / He / She / We are skiing	Il / eh – l
Nous skions	We ski / We are skiing	N – oo
Vous skiez	You ski / You are skiing	V – oo
Ils / Elles skient	They ski / They are skiing	Il / eh - l

Verb	Meaning	Pronunciation
Arriver	To come	Aa – ri – vay
j'arrive	I come / I am coming	J – aa – ri – v
tu arrives	You come / You are coming	T – u aa – ri – v
il/elle/on arrive	He / she / we come / he / she /we are coming	Il / eh – l aa – ri – v
nous arrivons	We come / We are coming	N – oo z aa – ri – vo
vous arrivez	You come / You are coming	V – oo z aa – ri – vay
ils / Elles arrivent	They come / They are coming	Il / eh – l z aa – ri – v

Verb	Meaning	Pronunciation
Danser	To dance	Do – n - say
je danse	I dance / I am dancing	J Do – n - s

tu danses	You / You are	T – u Do – n - s
il/elle / On danse	He/ she / we / he / she / we are	Il / eh – l / oh Do – n - s
nous dansons	We / We are	N – oo Do – n - so
vous dansez	You / You are	V – oo Do – n - say
ils / Elles dansent	They / They are	Il / eh – l Do – n - s

Verb	Meaning	Pronunciation
Chercher	To search	Sh – eh – r – sh - ay
je cherche	I search / I am searching	J sh – eh – r – sh
tu churches	You search / You are searching	T – u sh – eh – r – sh
il/elle/on cherche	He/ she / we search / he / she / we are searching	Il / eh – l /oh sh – eh – r – sh
nous cherchons	We search / We are searching	N – oo sh – eh – r – sh – o
vous cherchez	You search / You are	V – oo sh – eh – r – sh – ay
ils/elles cherchent	They search / They are	Il / eh – l sh – eh – r – sh

Verb	Meaning	Pronunciation
Fêter	To party / To celebrate	F – eh – tay
je fête	I party / I am partying	J f – eh – t
tu fêtes	You party / You are partying	T – u f – eh – t

il/elle/on fête	He/ she / we party / he / she / we are partying	Il / eh − l /oh f − eh − t
nous fêtons	We party / We are partying	N − oo z f − eh − t − o
vous fêtez	You party / You are partying	V − oo z f − eh − t − ez
ils/elles fêtent	They party / They are partying	Il / eh − l f − eh − t

Verb	Meaning	Pronunciation
Étudier	To study	Ay − tu − di − ay
j'étudie	I study / I am studying	J ay − tu − di
tu étudies	You study / You are studying	T − u ay − tu − di
il/elle étudie	He/ she / we study / he / she / we are studying	Il / eh − l / oh ay − tu − di
nous étudions	We study / We are studying	N − oo z ay − tu − di − o
vous étudiez	You study / You are studying	V − oo z ay − tu − di − ay
ils/elles étudient	They study / They are studying	Il / eh − l ay − tu − di

The Irregular Verbs (Les Verbes Irréguliers)

The verbs that do not end with "er" are the irregular verbs.

Verb	Meaning	Pronunciation
Être	To be	Eh − thr
je suis	I am	J s − u - i
tu es	You are	T − u ay
il/elle/on est	He / she / we are	Il / eh − l/oh ay

nous sommes	We are	N – oo s – o - m
vous êtes	You are	V – oo z eh – th
ils/elles sont	They are	Il / eh – l s – oh

Verb	Meaning	Pronunciation
Aller	To go	Aa - lay
je vais	I go / I am going	J vay
tu vas	You go / You are going	T – u vaa
il/elle va	He/ she / we go / he / she / we are going	Il / eh – l / oh vaa
nous allons	We go / We are going	N – oo z aa – lo
vous allez	You go / You are going	V – oo z aa – lay
ils/elles vont	They go / They are going	Il / eh – l vo

Verb	Meaning	Pronunciation
Avoir	To have	Aa – v – wa - r
j'ai	I have	J ay
tu as	You have	T – u aa
il/elle/on a	He/ she / we have	Il / eh – l / oh aa
nous avons	We have	N – oo z aa – vo
vous avez	You have	V – oo z aa – vay
ils/elles ont	They have	Il / eh – l z o

Verb	Meaning	Pronunciation
Faire	To do / To make	Fay – r
je fais	I do / I make / I am doing / I am making	J f – ay

tu fais	You do / You make / You are doing / You are making	T – u f - ay
il/elle/on fait	He/she/we make / he/she/we do / he/she/we are making / he/she/we are doing	Il / eh – l f - ay
nous faisons	We do / we make / we are doing / we are making	N – oo f – ay – z – o
vous faites	You do / You make / You are doing / You are making	V – oo f – eh – t
ils/elles font	They do / they make / they are doing / they are making	Il / eh – l f – o

Let us see a simple conversation between friends to understand how the verbs are used. Because it is between friends, it is going to be **an informal conversation**:

- Salut Maria

(s – eh – l – u m – aa – r – i - aa)

Hi Maria

- Salut David

(s – eh – l – u d – aa – vi – d)

Hi David

- Comment vas tu?

(k – o – m – o va t – u)

How are you?

- Ça va. Et toi?

(sa va ay t - wa)

Fine. And you?

- Moi aussi. Qu'est-ce que tu fais au soir?

(m – wa o – si k – eh – s – k t – u f – ay o s – wa – r)

Me too. What are you doing in the evening?

- Je vais au restaurant avec ma famille. C'est l'anniversaire de ma mère.

(j v – ay o r – eh – s – t – o – r – o aa – v – eh – k m – aa f – aa m – i say laa – ni – v – uh – r – s – eh – r d maa m – eh - r)

I am going to the restaurant with my family. It is my mother's birthday.

- D'accord. Félicitations. Amuse-toi.

(daa – k – o – r f – eh – li – si – taa – si – o aa – m – u – z t – wa)

Ok. Congratulations. Have fun.

- Oui. Merci

(vi m-eh – r - si)

Yes. Thank you

- Tu viens chez moi pendant le weekend? Noura et Fabio viennent samedi matin.

(t – u vi – ah sh – ay m – wa p – o – n – d – o l – uh vi – k – eh – n – d? n – oo – ra ay f – aa – b – I o vi – eh – n saa – m – di maa – t - ah)

You are coming to my place on the weekend? Noura and Fabio are coming Saturday morning.

- Oui. Bien sûr, mais je peux venir à l'après-midi parce que j'ai une classe de danse pendant le matin.

(vi bi – ah s – u – r m – eh j p – uh v – ni – r aa laa – p – r – eh mi – di paa – r – say – k j – ay u – n k – laa – s d d – o – n – s p – o – n – d – o l – uh maa – t – ah)

Yes. Of course, but I can come in afternoon because I have a dance class in the morning.

- Ça va. Pas de problème. Alors, tu peux apporter un gâteau avec toi? C'est l'anniversaire de Noura et il y a une boulangerie près de ta maison.

(saa vaa. Paa d p – r – oh – b leh – m aa – l – o r t – u p – uh aa – po – r – tay uh gaa – t – o aa – veh – k t – wa? Say laa – ni – v – uh – r – seh – r d n – oo ra ay i – l i - ya u – n b – oo – l – o – n – jay – ri p – r – eh d - taa may - zo)

Fine. No Problem. So, can you bring a cake with you? It is Noura's birthday and there is a bakery near your house.

- Oui. D'accord. Je dois apporter le gâteau au chocolat ou le gâteau aux fruits?

(vi. daa – ko – r. j d – wa aa – po – r – tay l gaa – to o sho – ko – laa oo l gaa – to o f – r – oo – i?)

Yes. Ok. Should I bring chocolate cake or fruit cake?

- Elle aime beaucoup le gâteau au chocolat.

(eh – l ey – m bo – k – oo l gaa – to o sho – ko – laa)

She really likes chocolate cake a lot.

- D'accord. Tu veux quelque autre chose?

(daa – ko – r. t – u v – uh k – eh – l – k o – th – r sho – z?)

Ok. Do you want something else?

- Non. Merci

(no. m – eh – r – si)

No. Thank you.

- Ahh.. c'est ça va. Alors à bientôt.

(aa…. Say sa va. Aa – lo – r aa bi – a – n – to)

Oh… Ok. So see you soon

- Oui à bientôt.

(vi aa bi – a – n – to)

Yes see you soon.

Exercise 1

Complete the following fill in the blanks with the conjugation of the verb given in brackets:

1. Tu _fais_ (faire) un bon café.
2. On _aime_ (aimer) les plages.
3. Paul _est_ (être) mon meilleur ami.
4. John et Carla _ont_ (avoir) beaucoup de voitures.
5. Ma maison _est_ (être) petite.
6. Je _quitte_ (quitter) mon travail car mon patron _est_ (être) impoli.
7. Nous _sauvons_ (sauver) des argents car nous voulons aller au voyage.
8. Tu peux _fermes_ (fermer) la porte?
9. Il _on accepte_ (accepter) ma proposition.
10. Je _____ (souhaiter) de te voir. _Souhaite_
11. Vous _louez_ (louer) un appartement ou une maison.
12. Nous _____ (pleurer) à cause de l'accident.
    pleurons

Exercise 2

Read the below passage and mark the correct response.

Antonio regarde un film le Dimanche. Il aime les films romantiques. Mais, son frère Devin déteste les films romantiques. Il aime écouter de la musique. Il cuisine un plat italian le dimanche. Il trouve cuisiner un plat chinois un peu difficile. Antonio ne cuisine pas. Son père est un enseignant de la langue japonaise. Il a 30 ans.

Question	Vrai (True)	Faux (False)	On ne sait pas (Not given)
Antonio aime cuisiner		✓	
Le père d'Antonio est japonaise		✓	
Antonio aime les sports			✓

Devin regarde un film le Dimanche			

Points To Remember

1. In the French language, there is no concept of the apostrophe. For example, if you want to say my friend's car. In French it will be "Car of my friend" i.e. La voiture de mon ami.
2. Also, the nouns are classified as masculine, feminine, and plural. For example: The word "door" in French is "Porte", which is a feminine noun.

Answer Key Chapter 1

Exercise 1

1. Fais (You make a good coffee)
2. Aime (We like beaches)
3. Est (Paul is my best friend)
4. Ont (John and Carla have a lot of cars)
5. Est (My house is small)
6. Quitte, est (I am quitting my work because my boss is rude)
7. Sauvons (We are saving money because we want to go to the trip)
8. Fermer (Csn you close the door?)
9. Accepte (He is accepting my proposal)
10. Souhaite (I wish to see you)
11. Louez (You are renting an apartment or a house)
12. Pleurons (We are crying because of the accident.)

Exercise 2

Antonio watches a movie on Sunday. He loves romantic movies. But, her brother Devin hates romantic movies. He likes listening to music. He cooks an Italian dish on Sundays. He finds cooking a Chinese dish a bit difficult. Antonio does not cook. Her father is a Japanese language teacher. He is 30 years old.

Question	Vrai (True)	Faux (False)	On ne sait pas (Not given)
Antonio aime cuisine		X	
Le père d'Antonio est japonaise		X	
Antonio aime les sports			X
Devin regarde un film le Dimanche			X

Chapter 2: Bonjour Mon Patron! (Hello My Boss !)

Verb Negations

Rule: Ne + verb (starting with consonant) + pas / N + verb (staring with vowel) + pas

Verb in positive conjugation	Verb in negative conjugation	Meaning in negative conjugation
Embaucher	Ne pas embaucher	To not hire
j'embauche	Je n'embauche pas	I am not hiring / I do not hire
tu embauches	tu n'embauches pas	You are not hiring / You do not hire
il/elle/on embauche	il/elle/on n'embauche pas	He/she/we are not hiring / He/she/we do not hire
nous embauchons	nous n'embauchons pas	We are not hiring / We do not hire
vous embauchez	vous n'embauchez pas	You are not hiring / You do not hire
ils/ells embauchent	ils/ells n'embauchent pas	They are not hiring / They do not hire

Verb in positive conjugation	Verb in negative conjugation	Meaning in negative conjugation
Virer	Ne pas virer	To not fire
je vire	Je ne vire pas	I do not fire / I am not firing
tu vires	tu ne vires pas	You do not fire / You are not firing
il/elle/on vire	il/elle/on ne vire pas	He/she/we do not fire / He/she/we are not firing
nous virons	nous ne virons pas	We do not fire / we are not firing
vous virez	vous ne virez pas	You do not fire / You are not firing
ils/elles virent	ils/elles ne virent pas	They do not fire / They are not firing

Verb in positive conjugation	Verb in negative conjugation	Meaning in negative conjugation
Travailler	Ne pas travailler	To not work
je travaille	je ne travaille pas	I do not work / I am not working
tu travailles	tu ne travailles pas	You do not work / You are not working
il/elle/on travaille	il/elle/on ne travaille pas	He/she/we do not work / He/she/we are not working
nous travaillons	nous ne travaillons pas	We do not work / We are not working
vous travaillez	vous ne travaillez pas	You do not work / You are not working

ils/elles travaillent	ils/elles ne travaillent pas	They do not work / They are not working

Verb in positive conjugation	Verb in negative conjugation	Meaning in negative conjugation
Offrir	Ne pas offrir	To not offer
j'offre	Je n'offre pas	I am not offering / I do not offer
tu offres	tu n'offres pas	You are not offering / You do not offer
il/elle/on offer	il/elle/on n'offre pas	He/She/We are not offering / He/she/we do not offer
nous offrons	nous n'offrons pas	We are not offering / We do not offer
vous offrez	vous n'offrez pas	You are not offering / You do not offer
ils/elles offrent	ils/elles n'offrent pas	They are not offering / They do not offer

Verb in positive conjugation	Verb in negative conjugation	Meaning in negative conjugation
Postuler	Ne pas postuler	To Not Apply
je postule	Je ne postule pas	I am not applying / I do not apply
tu postules	tu ne postules pas	You are not applying / You do not apply

il/elle /on postule	il/elle/on ne postule pas	He / She / We are not applying / He/She/We do not apply
nous postulons	Nous ne postulons pas	We are not applying / We do not apply
vous postulez	Vous ne postulez pas	You are not applying / You do not apply
ils/elles postulant	ils/elles ne postulent pas	They are not applying / They do not apply

Vocabulary (Relating to the Work)

Word	Meaning	Pronunciation
Le métier	occupation	L – uh m – ay – ti – ay
Le boulot	work – informal	L – uh b – oo – lo
Le travail	Work	L – uh thr – va – ay
L'emploi	employment	L – o – m – p – l – wa
Le poste	post, position	L – uh po – s – t
La carrière	career	Laa ka – ri – eh – r
La vocation	vocation	Laa vo – ka – si – o
L'opportunité d'emploi	job opportunity	Lo – po – r – tu – ni – tay
Le stage en enterprise	internship	L – uh s – taa – j o – no –n – thr – pri – z
Le taf	work – slang	L – uh taa – f

Bosser	to work – casual	Bo – s – ay
Travailler	to work	Thr – a – vi – ay
Gérer	to manage	Jay – ray
Bosser comme un âne	to work like too much / to work like a dog (informal)	Bo – s – ay ko – m uh – n – aa – n
Travailler dur	to work hard	Thr – aa – vi – ay d – u – r
Bien travailler	to work well	Bi – ah thr – aa – vaa – i – ay
la tâche	Task	Laa – taa – sh
Pièces jointes	Attachments	Pi – eh – s j – wa – n – t
la pause café	coffee break	Laa – po – z kaa – fay
Le chef	The head	L – uh sh – eh – f
le chômage	Unemployment	L – uh – sh – o – maa – j
Ordinateur	Computer	O – r – di – naa – t – uh – r
l'emploi	Employment	Lo – m – pl – wa
Écouteurs	Headphones	Ay – k – oo – t – uh – r
le congé	holiday, leave	L – uh ko – n – jay
Clavier	Keyboard	K – laa – vi – ay
le salarié	employee	L – uh saa – laa – ri – ay
Équipe	Team	Ay – ki – p
le patron	Boss	L – uh – paa – t – ro
le collègue	coworker	L – uh k – o – l – eh – j
le bureau	office	L – uh b – u – ro

le contrat	Contract	L – uh k – on – t – ra
la reunion	Reunion	L – uh r – ay – uni – o
la formation	Training	Laa fo – r – maa – si – oh
embaucher / Engager	to hire	Oh – m – bo – sh – ay / oh – gaa – jay
la gestion	management	Laa j – eh – s – ti – o
Terminer	to finish	T – eh – r – mi – nay
Le dossier	file	L – uh do – si – ay
l'entretien	interview	Lo – n – thr – ti – ah
les ragots	gossip	Lay – raa – go
Bavarder	to chat	Baa – vaa – r – day
la grève	Strike	Laa g – r – eh – v
la manifestation	demonstration	Laa maa – ni – f – eh – s – ta – si - oh
les syndicats	trade-union	Lay si – n – di – kaa
le treizième mois	Year end bonus	L – uh thr – eh – zi – eh – m m – wa
CDD (Contract Duration Determinée)	fixed-term contract on a short term basis	Say d-ay d-ay
CDI (Contract Duration Indeterminée)	open-ended contract	Say d-ay ee

The Numbers (Les Nombres)

0	Zéro	Zay - ro
1	Un	uh
2	Deux	D – uh
3	Trois	Thr - wa
4	Quatre	K – eh – th – r
5	Cinq	Sank
6	Six	See – s
7	Sept	S – eh – th
8	Huit	Wee – th
9	Neuf	N – f
10	Dix	D – ee – s
11	Onze	Oh – n – z
12	Douze	D – oo – z
13	Treize	Thr – eh – z
14	Quatorze	Ka – to – r – z
15	Quinze	K – eh – n – z
16	Seize	S – eh – z
17	Dix – sept	Dee – z – s – eh – th
18	Dix – huit	Dee – z – wee – th
19	Dix - neuf	Dee – z – n – f
20	Vingt	V – ah
21	Vingt – et - un	V – ah – t – ay – uh
22	Vingt - deux	V – ah – d – uh
23	Vingt - trois	V – ah – thr – wa
24	Vingt - quatre	V – ah – k – eh – th – r
25	Vingt - cinq	V – ah – sank
26	Vingt – six	V – ah – see – s
27	Vingt - sept	V – ah – s – eh – th
28	Vingt - huit	V – ah – wee – th
29	Vingt - neuf	V – ah – n – f

30	Trente	Thr – on – t
31	Trente - et - un	Thr – on – t – ay – uh
32	Trente - deux	Thr – on – t – d – uh
33	Trente - trois	Thr – on – t – thr – wa
34	Trente - quatre	Thr – on – t – k – eh – thr
35	Trente - cinq	Thr – on – t - sank
36	Trente - six	Thr – on – th – see – s
37	Trente - sept	Thr – on – th – s – eh – th
38	Trente - huit	Thr – on – th – wee – th
39	Trente - neuf	Thr – on – th – n – f
40	Quarante	K – eh – ro – n – t
41	Quarante – et - un	K – eh – ro – n – t – ay – uh
42	Quarante – deux	K – eh – ro – n – t – d – uh
43	Quarante – trois	K – eh – ro – n – t – thr – wa
44	Quarante - quatre	K – eh – ro – n – t – k – eh – thr
45	Quarante - cinq	K – eh – ro – n – t – sank
46	Quarante – six	K – eh – ro – n – t – see – s
47	Quarante - sept	K – eh – ro – n – t – s – eh – th
48	Quarante - huit	K – eh – ro – n – t – wee – th
49	Quarante - neuf	K – eh – ro – n – t – n – f
50	Cinquante	Sank – on – t
51	Cinquante – et – un	Sank – on – tay – uh
52	Cinquante – deux	Sank – on – t – d – uh
53	Cinquante – trois	Sank – on – t – thr – wa
54	Cinquante - quatre	Sank – on – t – k – eh – thr
55	Cinquante - cinq	Sank – on – t – sank
56	Cinquante - six	Sank – on – t – see – s
57	Cinquante – sept	Sank – on – t – s – eh – th
58	Cinquante-huit	Sank – on – t – sank
59	Cinquante – neuf	Sank – on – t – n – f

60	Soixante	Swa – son – t
61	Soixante - et – un	Swa – son – tay – uh
62	Soixante – deux	Swa – son – t – d – uh
63	Soixante - trois	Swa – son – t – thr – wa
64	Soixante – quatre	Swa – son – t – k – eh – thr
65	Soixante - cinq	Swa – son – t – sank
66	Soixante – six	Swa – son – t – see – s
67	Soixante - sept	Swa – son – t – s – eh – th
68	Soixante - huit	Swa – son – t – wee – th
69	Soixante - neuf	Swa – son – t – n – f
70	Soixante - dix	Swa – son – t – dee – z
71	Soixante - et - onze	Swa – son – tay – on – z
72	Soixante – douze	Swa – son – t – d – oo – z
73	Soixante - treize	Swa – son – t – thr – eh – z
74	Soixante - quatorze	Swa – son – t – kaa – to – rz
75	Soixante – quinze	Swa – son – t – keh – n - z
76	Soixante - seize	Swa – son – t – seh - z
77	Soixante - dix - sept	Swa – son – t – dee – z – seh – th
78	Soixante - dix - huit	Swa – son – t – dee – z – wee - th
79	Soixante - dix - neuf	Swa – son – t – dee – z – n – f
80	Quatre - vingts	Keh – thr – va - n
81	Quatre - vingt – un	Keh – thr – va – n - uh
82	Quatre - vingt - deux	Keh – thr – va – n – d – uh
83	Quatre - vingt - trois	Keh – thr – va – n – thr – wa
84	Quatre – vingt – quatre	Keh – thr – va – n – keh – thr
85	Quatre - vingt - cinq	Keh – thr – va – n – sank

86	Quatre - vingt - six	Keh – thr – va – n – see – s
87	Quatre – vingt - sept	Keh – thr – va – n – seh – th
88	Quatre - vingt - huit	Keh – thr – va – n – wee – th
89	Quatre – vingt - neuf	Keh – thr – va – n – n – f
90	Quatre - vingt - dix	Keh – thr – va – n – dee – z
91	Quatre - vingt – onze	Keh – thr – va – n – oh - n – z
92	Quatre - vingt - douze	Keh – thr – va – n – doo – z
93	Quatre – vingt - treize	Keh – thr – va – n – thr – eh – z
94	Quatre - vingt – quatorze	Keh – thr – va – n – kaa – to – rz
95	Quatre – vingt - quinze	Keh – thr – va – n – keh – nz
96	Quatre - vingt - seize	Keh – thr – va – n – seh – z
97	Quatre – vingt – dix – sept	Keh – thr – va – n – deez – seh – th
98	Quatre - vingt - dix - huit	Keh – thr – va – n – deez – wee - th
99	Quatre – vingt – dix – neuf	Keh – thr – va – n – deez – n – f
100	Cent	S - oh
101	Cent – un	S – oh – uh
107	Cent – septh	S – oh – seh – th
200	Deux – cents	D – uh - S – oh
250	Deux – cent – cinquante	D – uh - S – oh – sank – on – th
300	Trois – cents	Thr – wa - s - oh
380	Trois – cent – quatre – vingt	Thr – wa – s - oh

500	Cinq – cents	Sank - s – oh
1000	Mille	Mi – l
1400	Mille – quatre – cents	Mi – l – keh – thr - s – oh
2550	Deux – mille – cinq – cent – cinquante	D – uh – mi – l – sank - s – oh – sank – on – t
10,000	Dix – milles	Dee – z – mi – l
100,000	Cent – milles	S – oh – mi - l
1000,000	Million	Mi – li – o

How to Ask for Help From Someone

Expression	Meaning	Pronunciation
Vous pourriez m'aider, s'il vous plaît?	Could you help me, please?	V – oo p – oo – ri – ay m – ey – d – ay si – l – v – oo – p – l –ay
Pouvez-vous me donner un coup de main?	Can you give me a hand? / Can you help me?	P – oo – vay v – oo m d – o – nay uh c – oo d m – ah
Pouvez-vous m'aider s'il vous plaît?	Can you help me please?	P – oo – vay v – oo m – eh – d – ay si – l – v – oo – p – l –ay
J'ai besoin de votre aide.	I need your help	J – ay b – s- wa d v – oh – th – r ey – d
Aidez-moi, s'il vous plaît.	Help me please.	Ay – d – ay m – wa si – l – v – oo – p – l –ay

Let Us See an Office Conversation Scenario

Salarié - Bonjour Monsieur, Paul est absent aujourd'hui parce que sa voiture est tombée en panne. Les autres sont tous présent.

(Employee - Hello Sir, Paul is absent today because his car broke down. The others are all present.)

Patron - D'accord. Paul est toujours absent et en plus il ne travaille pas bien depuis 3 mois. Je n'ai pas d'autre choix que de le mettre en préavis. Côte à côte, vous pouvez commencer trouver un nouveau employé. Nous allons embaucher une personne parce qu'il y a de nouveaux projets.

(Boss - Okay. Paul is always absent and on top of that he hasn't working well for 3 months. I have no choice but to put him on notice. Side by side, you can start finding a new employee. We are going to hire someone because there are new projects.)

Salarié - D'accord. Je vais mettre une annonce en ligne.

(Employee - Okay. I will put an advertisement online.)

Patron - Bon. David, vous travaillez très fort. Vous complétez toutes vos tâches à l'heure, Alors, je voudrais vous offrir la promotion.

(Boss - Good. David, you work very hard. You complete all your tasks on time, So I would like to offer you the promotion.)

Salarié - Merci beaucoup monsieur. Vous m'encouragez de faire mon meilleur.

(Employee - Thank you very much sir. You encourage me to do my best.)

Patron - Félicitations, ce sont vos efforts.

(Boss - Congratulations, it's your efforts.)

Salarié - Je vous remercie Monsieur

(Employee - Thank you Mister)

Patron - Je vous en prie. Envoyez-moi la liste des employés avant la fin de la journée.

(Boss - Please. Send me the list of employees before the end of the day.)

Salarié - Oui. D'accord.

(Employee - Yes. OK.)

Exercise 1

Write the negatives of the following sentences:

1. Je suis occupé aujourd'hui.
2. Paul a quinze ans.
3. Vous voulez faire mon devoir.
4. Nous embauchons un enseignant de la langue espagnole
5. L'entreprise vire 12 employés.
6. Mon patron peut offrir un emploi à David.
7. Tu postule pour ce travail.
8. Vous êtes triste à cause de moi
9. Nous travaillons à Paris
10. J'aime la pluie.

Exercise 2

Write the following numbers in words:

1. 654,976
2. 90,086
3. 5,754,245
4. 12,758,457
5. 75,976
6.   8,950

Exercise 3

Write the opposite of the following words

1. Embaucher
2. Augmenter
3. Engager
4. Aimer
5. Aller
6. Naître

Points To Remember

1. When making the negative of a sentence with a quantity, the quantity is changed to "de". For example: J'ai une voiture changes to Je n'ai pas de voiture. (I have a car changes to I don't have a car.)

2. When making the negative of a sentence with the definite articles (le, la, les, l'), the definite article do not change. For example: Nous adorons les montagnes changes to Nous n'adorons pas les montagnes. (We love mountains changes to we don't love mountains.)

3. The number one with masculine nouns is "un" and with a feminine noun it's "une". For example: Un problème (A problem); Une chaise (A chair)

Answer Key Chapter 2

Exercise 1

1. Je ne suis pas occupé aujourd'hui.
2. Paul n'a pas quinze ans.
3. Vous ne voulez pas faire mon devoir.
4. Nous n'embauchons pas d'enseignant de la langue espagnole
5. L'entreprise ne vire pas d'employés.
6. Mon patron ne peut pas offrir un emploi à David.
7. Tu ne postule pas pour ce travail.
8. Vous n'êtes pas triste à cause de moi
9. Nous ne travaillons pas à Paris
10. Je n'aime pas la pluie.

Exercise 2

1. Six – cent – cinquante – quatre – mille – neuf – cent – soixante – seize
2. Quatre – vingt – dix – mille – quatre – vingt – six
3. Cinq – million – sept – cent – cinquante – quatre – mille – deux – cent – quarante – cinq
4. Douze – million – sept – cent – cinquante – huit – mille – quatre – cent – cinquante – sept
5. Soixante – quinze – mille – neuf – cent – soixante – seize
6. Huit – mille – neuf – cent – cinquante

Exercise 3

1. Virer (To fire)
2. Diminuer (To decrease)
2. Virer (To fire)
3. Détester (To hate)
4. Venir (To come)
5. Mourir (To Die)

Chapter 3: Acheter un cadeau (To Buy a Gift)

Vocabulary

Word	Meaning	Pronunciation
Un kilo d'oranges	A kilo of oranges	Uh – ki – lo – d – oh – ron – j
Un kilo de tomates	A kilo of tomatoes	Uh – ki – lo – d – to – maa – t
Un kilo de carottes	A kilo of carrots	Uh – ki – lo – d – kaa – ro – t
Une boîte de fraises	A box of strawberries	U – n – bwa – t – d – f – reh – z
Une boîte de champignons	A box of mushrooms	U – n - bwa – t – d – sh – om – pi – ni – o
Un melon	A melon	Uh – meh – lo
Un kilo de citron	A kilo of lemons	Uh – ki – lo - d – si – t – ro
Une douzaine de bananes	A dozen of bananas	U – n – doo – z – eh – n – d – baa – naa – n
Une bouteille de vin	A bottle of wine	U – n – boo – t – uh – i – d – v – ah
Un pot de confiture	A can of jam	Uh – po – d – co – fi – t – u – r
Un cube de beurre	A cube of butter	Uh – k – u – b – d – b – uh – r
Un litre de lait	A liter of milk	Uh – li – th – r – d – lay
Un verre de jus d'orange	A glass of orange juice	Uh – veh – r – d – ju – d – oh – ron – j

Un paquet de jus de fruit	A packet of orange juice	Uh – paa – keh – t – d – ju – d – f – ru – i
Un paquet de sucre	A packet of sugar	Uh – paa – keh – t – d – s – u – k - uh – r
Une boîte de chocolat	A box of chocolate	U – n – bwa – t – d – sh – o – ko – laa
Un gâteau au chocolat	A chocolate cake	Uh – gaa – to – o – sh – o – ko – laa
Un gâteau aux fraises	A strawberries cake	Uh – gaa – to – o – f – reh – z
Un croissant	A croissant	Uh – k – rwa – so
Une baguette	A baguette	U – n – baa – g – eh – th
Un paquet de pain	A packet of bread	Uh – paa – keh – t – d – p – aah
Un paquet de biscuit	A packet of biscuit	Uh – paa – keh – t – d – bi – s – ku – i
Un stylo rouge	A red pen	Uh – sti – lo – roo – j
Un stylo bleu	A blue pen	Uh – sti – lo – b – l – uh
Un stylo noir	A black pen	Uh – sti – lo – nwa – r
Un crayon	A pencil	Uh – k – ra – yo
Un taille-crayon	A sharpner	Uh – taa – I – k – ra – yo.
Un dictionnaire	A dictionary	Uh – di – k – si – o – n – ay – r
Un cahier	A notebook	Uh – ka – i – ay
Un classeur	A workbook (a spiral binded notebook)	Uh – k – laa – s – r
Un livre	A book	Uh – li – v – r
Une feutre	A marker	U – n – f – n – eh – t – r

Une craie	A chalk	U – n – k – ray
Des antibiotiques	Antibiotics	D – ay – on – ti – bi – o – ti – k
Une pomade	An ointment	U – n – po – maa – d
Des savons	Soaps	D – ay – saa – vo
Du coton	Cotton	Du – ko – to
Une pâte dentifrice	A toothpaste	U – n – paa – t – d – on – ti – fri – s
Des médicaments	Medication	D – ay – may – di – kaa – mo
Une tasse	A cup	U – n – taa – s
Une porte-clé	A keychain	U o n – po – r – t – k – lay
Un parfum	A perfume	Uh – paa – r – fa
Un cadre de photo	A photo frame	Uh – kaa - d – r – d – fo – to
Un pansement	A bandage	Uh – p – on – z – mo
Un sandwich	A sandwich	Uh – s – on – d – vi – ch
Une assiette de pâtes	A plate of pasta	U – n – aa – si – eh – t – d – paa – t
Un verre de thé glace	A glass of iced tea	Uh – v – eh – r – d – tay – g – laa – s
Un pantaloons	A pantaloons	Uh – paa – n – taa – lo
Une jupe	A skirt	U – n – ju – p
Un foulard	Scarf	Uh – foo – laa – r
Une paire de chaussures	A pair of shoes	U – n – p – ay – r – d – sho – si – u – r
Une chemise	A shirt	U – n – sh – mi – z

Example of a Conversation (Buying a Gift From a Shop)

Vendeur - Bonjour Madame. Comment je peux vous aider?

(Salesman - Hello Madam. How can I help you?)

Cliente - Bonjour, je cherche un cadeau pour mon meilleur ami, c'est son anniversaire.

(Client - Hello, I'm looking for a present for my best friend, it's his birthday.)

Vendeur - D'accord madame. Quel type de cadeau cherchez-vous?

(Salesman - Okay ma'am. What type of gift are you looking for?)

Cliente - Il aime beaucoup des choses antiques. Pouvez-vous montrer quelque chose d'antique?

(Client - He likes antique things a lot. Can you show something antique?)

Vendeur - Oui madame. Voici, une montre ancienne, son design est très unique.

(Salesman - Yes ma'am. Here is an old watch, its design is very unique.)

Cliente - C'est bon. Mais il a déjà ces montres.

(Client - It's okay. But he already has these watches.)

Vendeur - D'accord Madame. Avez-vous pensé à quelque chose que vous voulez offrir?

(Salesman - Ok ma'am. Have you thought of something you want to give as a gift?)

Cliente - Non, c'est très de trancher. Mais il aime l'appareil photo. Avez-vous un appareil photo ancien?

(Client - No, it's a big deal. But he loves the camera. Do you have an antique camera?)

Vendeur - Oui Madame. Voilà

(Salesman - Yes Madam. Here it is.)

Cliente - C'est beau. Ça coûte combien?

(Client - It's beautiful. How much does it cost?)

Vendeur - Ça coûte 500 euro madame.

(Salesman - It costs 500 euro madam.)

Cliente - Oh là là. C'est très cher. Pouvez-vous offrir une remise?

(Client - Oh dear. It is very expensive. Can you offer a discount?)

Vendeur - Oui Madame, Heureusement cet appareil photo est en remise. Ça coûtera 350 euros après remise.

(Salesman - Yes Madam, Fortunately this camera is on discount. It will cost 350 euros after discount.)

Cliente - C'est excellent. Alors je voudrais acheter cet appareil photo. Pouvez-vous également l'emballer?

(Client - This is excellent. So I would like to buy this camera. Can you also pack it?)

Vendeur - Oui madame. Bien sûr.

(Salesman - Yes ma'am. Sure.)

Cliente - Comment je peux vous payer? En espèces ou par la carte bancaire?

(Client - How can I pay you? In cash or by credit card?)

Vendeur - Comme vous voulez madame. Nous acceptons les deux modes de paiement.

(Salesman - As you wish ma'am. We accept both payment methods.)

Cliente - Voilà ma carte bancaire.

(Client - Here is my bank card.)

Vendeur - Merci madame. Bonne journée.

(Salesman - Thank you ma'am. Good day.)

Cliente - Merci. Au revoir.

(Client - Thank you. Bye.)

Irregular Verbs Conjugation

Verb	Meaning	Pronunciation
Offrir	To offer	O – f – ri – r
J'offre	I offer / I am offering	Jo – f – r
Tu offres	You offer / You are offering	T – u - o – f - r
Il / Elle / On offre	He / She / We offer / He / She / We are offering	Il / eh – l / oh o – f - r
Nous offrons	We offer / We are offering	N – oo z o – f – ro
Vous offrez	You offer / You are offering	V – oo z o – f – ray
Ils / Elles offrent	They offer / They are offering	Il / eh – l z o – f – r

Verb	Meaning	Pronunciation
Vendre	To sell	V – on – d – r
Je vends	I sell / I am selling	J v – oh
Tu vends	You sell / You are selling	T – u v – oh
Il / Elle / On vend	He / She / We sell / He / She / We are selling	Il / eh – l / oh v - oh
Nous vendons	We sell / We are selling	N – oo v – oh d – oh
Vous vendez	You sell / You are selling	V – oo v – oh – d – ay
Ils / Elles vendent	They sell / They are selling	Il / eh – l v – oh - d

Verb	Meaning	Pronunciation
Obtenir	To get	O – b – t – ni – r
J'obtiens	I get / I am getting	Jo – b – ti - ah
Tu obtiens	You get / You are getting	T – u o – b – ti – ah
Il / Elle / On obtient	He / She / We get / He / She / We are getting	Il / eh – l / oh o – b – ti – ah
Nous obtenons	We get / We are getting	N – oo – z – o – b – t - no
Vous obtenez	You get / You are getting	V – oo – z – o – t – nay
Ils / Elles obtiennent	They get / They are getting	Il / eh – l - z – o – b – ti – eh – n

Verb	Meaning	Pronunciation
Prendre	To take	P – ro – n – d – r
Je prends	I take / I am taking	J – p – r - oh
Tu prends	You take / You are taking	T – u – p – r - oh
Il / Elle / On prend	He / She / We take / He / She / We are taking	Il / eh – l / oh – p – r - oh
Nous prenons	We take / We are taking	N – oo – p – r – uh – no
Vous prenez	You take / You are taking	V – oo – p – r – uh – nay
Ils / Elles prennent	They take / They are taking	Il / eh – l – p – r – eh - n

Les Adjectifs Possessifs (Possessive Adjectives)

Possessive adjectives are used to express a possession of a noun. For example: My books, His car, etc.

The gender of Possessive adjectifs depends on the gender of the noun. For example: Voiture is a feminine noun so it can come with Ma, Ta, Sa, Votre, Notre, Leur. Ma Voiture (My Car), Ta voiture (Your car), Sa voiture (His/ her car), Votre voiture (Your car), Notre voiture (Our car), Leur voiture (Their car).

Masculine Possessive adjectives	Pronunciation	Feminine Possessive adjectives	Pronunciation	Plural Possessive adjectives	Pronunciation	Meaning
Mon	M – oh	Ma	M – aa	Mes	M – ay	My
Ton	T – oh	Ta	T – aa	Tes	T – ay	Your
Son	S – oh	Sa	S – aa	Ses	S – ay	His / Her
Votre	V – oh – th – r	Votre	V – oh – th – r	Vos	V – oh	Your
Notre	No – th – r	Notre	No – th – r	Nos	N – o	Our
Leur	L – uh – r	Leur	L – uh – r	Leurs	L – uh – r	Their

Note: Before a noun that starts with a vowel, we always use masculine possessive adjective. For example: Mon amie (However, amie is feminine, but as it starts with a vowel, so we use masculine possessive adjective.

The Directions (Les Directions)

Direction	Meaning	Pronunciation
À droite	On the right	Aa – d – rwa – t
À gauche	On the left	Aa – go – sh
Tout droit	Straight	T – ooo – d – rwa
La première rue à droite	The first street on the right	Laa – p – r – mi – eh – r - r – u - aa – d – rwa – t
La troisième rue à gauche	The third street on the left	Laa – th – rwa – si – eh – m - r – u - aa – go – sh
La rue suivante	The next street	Laa - r – u – s – ooo – i – vo – n – t
En face de	In front of	Oh – faa – s – d
À côté de	Next to	Aa – k – o – tay – d
Au bout de la rue	At the end of the street	O – b – ooo – d – laa – r – u

Exercise 1

Choose the right option:

1. Vous avez (votre / ton / ta) livre?
2. Ma sœur a (son / sa / ses) cadeaux.
3. (Notre / Nos / Ta) parents habitent avec nous à Paris.
4. Tu vas aller chez (ton / ta / mes) grand-mère pour (tes/ ses/ ton) vacances d'été.
5. (Leur / leurs / mon) fille vient chez eux le samedi.
6. (Mon / Ma / Mes) amie Carla habite en France sans ses parents.

Exercise 2

Choose the right option:

1. J'achète (un / une) parfum pour toi de France.
2. Nous avons (un / une) nouveau porte-clés parce que nous avons perdu autre porte-clés.
3. (Le/La) magasin offre (un / une) échantillon gratuit de champagne.
4. (Un / une) étudiante lit (le / la) roman du célèbre auteur français.
5. (La / Le) maison a (une / un) chambre, (un / une) cuisine et (un / une) salon.

Exercise 3

Complete the sentences with the conjugation of the verbs in brackets:

1. Elle _____ (aller) au marché avec son amie Carla.
2. Tu _____ (avoir) une surprise pour lui.
3. Daniel et Laura _____ (vendre) leur appartement.
4. Vous _____ (prendre) une tasse de café.
5. Nous _____ (offrir) une remise de 5 pourcent si vous acheter plus de 5 chemises.

Answer Key Chapter 3

Exercise 1

1. Votre
2. Ses
3. Nos
4. Ta, tes
6. Leur
7. Ma

Exercise 2

1. Un
2. Un
3. Le, un
4. Une, le
5. La, une, une, un

Exercise 3

1. Va
2. As
3. Vendent
4. Prenez
6. Offrons

Chapter 4: Allons au travail (Let's Go To Work)

Word	Meaning	Pronunciation
Embaucher	To fire (verb)	Om – bo – sh – ay
Engager	To hire (verb)	On – gaa – j – ay
Virer	To fire (verb)	Vi – ray
Employé(e)	Employee	Om – p – lo – i – ay
Employeur	Employer	Om – p – lo – i – uh – r
Bureau	Office	Bu – ro
Entretien	Interview	On – thr – ti – ah
Postuler	To apply	Po – s – tu – lay
Emploi	Job	Om – p – lwa
Métier	Profession	May – ti – ay
Formulaire	Form	Foh - r – mu – lay – r
Formation	Training	Fo – maa – si – o
Chômage	Unemployment	Sh – o – maa – g
Un emploi à temps plein	A full-time job	Uh – n – om – p – lwa
Un travail à temps-partiel	A part-time job	Uh – thr – vaa – ay
Un salaire	Salary	Uh – saa – lay – r
Quitter	To quit	Ki – tay
Démissionner	To resign	D – ay – mi – si – o – nay
Heures supplémentaires	Overtime	Uh – r – su – p – li – m - on – tay – r
CV (Resume)	Curriculum vitae	Ku – ri – ku – lum - vi – tay
Stagiaire	Trainee	Staa – jay – r
Stage	Internship	Staa – j

Un poste à pourvoir	A vacancy	
L'expérience professionnelle	Work experience	
Carrière	Career	
Offre d'emploi	Job advertisement	

Example of a Conversation (Between 2 Colleagues)

Michel - Bonjour Valerie

(Michel - Hello Valerie)

Valerie- Bonjour Michel. Comment vas tu?

(Valerie- Hello Michel. How are you doing?)

Michel - Ça va très bien. Et toi?

(Michel – I am doing very well. And you?)

Valerie- Oui, je vais bien aussi. Tu as l'air d'être vraiment heureux. Qu'est-ce qui s'est passé?

(Valerie- Yes, I'm fine too. You seem to be really happy. What happened?)

Michel - Oui. Aujourd'hui, le chef de mon département a annoncé une bonne nouvelle. Il m'offre une promotion.

(Michel - Yes. Today the head of my department announced some good news. He's offering me a promotion.)

Valerie- C'est fantastique! On doit célébrer.

(Valerie- It's fantastic! We have to celebrate.)

Michel - Oui. Alors tu as postulé pour le poste à pouvoir chez Infotech?

(Michel - Yes. So you applied for the current position at Infotech?)

Valerie- Oui. J'ai un entretien demain. Je suis un peu nerveuse.

(Valerie- Yes. I have an interview tomorrow. I'm a little nervous.)

Michel - Ne t'inquiète pas. Tu es très intelligente. Tu vas obtenir cet emploi.

(Michel - Don't worry. You are very smart. You are going to get this job.)

Valerie- J'espère que j'obtiens cet emploi parce que c'est une bonne entreprise.

(Valerie- Hope I get this job because it's a good company.)

Michel - Bonne chance. Tu as entendu que Daniel avait démissionné?

(Michel - Good luck. Did you hear Daniel quit?)

Valerie - Oui. C'est une triste nouvelle. Il a travaillé ici pendant 10 ans.

(Valerie - Yes. This is sad news. He worked here for 10 years.)

Daniel - Oui. Avec son expérience de travail, il envisage d'ouvrir sa propre entreprise.

(Daniel - Yes. With his work experience, he plans to open his own business.)

Valerie - C'est bon. Je dois préparer pour mon entretien. Alors, à bientôt.

(Valerie – It is good. I have to prepare for my interview. So see you soon.)

Daniel - Au revoir.

(Daniel - Goodbye.)

Verbs and Their Conjugation (Relation to the Work Environment)

Verb	Meaning	Pronunciation
Soumettre	To submit	S – oo – m – eh – th - r
Je soumets	I submit / I am submitting	J – s – oo – m – ay
Tu soumets	You submit / You are submitting	T – u – s – oo – m – ay
Il / Elle / On soumet	He / She / We submit / He / She / We are submitting	Il / eh – l / oh – s – oo – m – ay
Nous soumettons	We submit / We are submitting	N – oo – s – oo – m – eh - to
Vous soumettez	You submit / You are submitting	V – oo – s – oo – m – eh - tay

Ils / Elles soumettent	They submit / They were submitting	Il / eh – l – s – oo – m – eh – t

Verb	Meaning	Pronunciation
Partager	To share	Paa – r – taa - jay
Je partage	I share / I am sharing	J – paa – r – taa – j
Tu partages	You share / You are sharing	T – u – paa – r – taa – j
Il / Elle / On partage	He / She / We share / He / She / We are sharing	Il / eh – l / oh – paa – r – taa - j
Nous partageons	We share / We are sharing	N – oo – paa – r – taa - jo
Vous partagez	You share / You are sharing	V – oo – paa – r – taa - jay
Ils / Elles partagent	They share / They are sharing	Il / eh – l – paa – r – taa – j

Verb	Meaning	Pronunciation
Soutenir	To support	S – oo – t – ni – r
Je soutiens	I support / I am supporting	J – s – oo – ti – ah
Tu soutiens	You support / You are supporting	T – u – s – oo – ti – ah
Il / Elle / On soutient	He / She / We support / He / She / We are supporting	Il / eh – l / oh – s – oo – ti – ah
Nous soutenons	We support / We are supporting	N – oo – s – oo – t - no
Vous soutenez	You support / You are supporting	V – oo – s – oo – t – nay

Ils / Elles soutiennent	They support / They are supporting	Il / eh – l – s – oo – ti – eh – n

Verb	Meaning	Pronunciation
Mettre	To put	M – eh – th – r
Je mets	I put / I am putting	J – m – ay
Tu mets	You put / You are putting	T – u – m – ay
Il / Elle / On met	He / She / We put / He / She / We are putting	Il / eh – l / oh – m - ay
Nous mettons	We put / We are putting	N – oo – m – eh – t – oh
Vous mettez	You put / You are putting	V – oo – m – eh – tay
Ils / Elles mettent	They put / They are putting	Il / eh – l – m – eh – t

The Future Tense (Le Future Proche)

The rule for formation of future tense is: The conjugation of the verb "aller" + the root form of the main verb.

For example, if we want to say: He will eat bread. The main verb is "eat", in French it is "manger". So the translation will be "Il va manger un pain."

Let us also quickly recall the conjugation of the verb "aller".

Aller
Je vais
Tu vas
Il / Elle / On va
Nous allons
Vous allez
Ils / Elles vont

Examples of Future Tense

Sentence in Present tense	Meaning	Sentence in Future tense	Meaning
Je partage ma nourriture avec mon frère	I share my food with my brother	Je vais partager ma nourriture avec mon frère	I will share my food with my brother
Nous venons au restaurant avec nos amis en voiture	We are coming to the restaurant with our friends by car.	Nous allons venir au restaurant avec nos amis en voiture	We will come to the restaurant with our friends by car
Elle écoute la musique de la classe.	She is listening to the music in the class.	Elle va écouter la musique de la classe.	She will listen to the music in the class
Ils montrent leur maison au vendeur du magasin près de chez eux.	They are showing their house to the salesperson from the shop near their house.	Ils vont montrer leur maison au vendeur du magasin près de chez eux.	They will show their house to the salesperson from the shop near their house.
Le train arrive à l'heure dans cette gare	The train comes on time at this railway station	Le train va arriver à l'heure dans cette gare	The train will come on time at this railway station
Les horaires sont fixes pour les cours de français.	The hours are fixed for the french classes.	Les horaires vont être fixes pour les cours de français.	The hours will be fixed for the french classes.
Nous allons du Canada aux États-Unis en avion.	We are going from Canada to U.S by airplane.	Nous allons aller du Canada aux États-Unis en avion.	We will go from Canada to U.S by airplane.

The Negative of Future Tense

The rule to make the negative of future tense is: subject + ne + the verb "aller" + pas + the root form of the main verb. Or, in other words, Ne + verb1 + pas + verb2

Examples of Negative of Future Tense

Positive Sentence in Future Tense	Meaning	Negative Sentence in Future Tense	Meaning
Le bus va partir demain à 17h de Paris	The bus will leave at 5pm from Paris tomorrow	Le bus ne va pas partir demain à 17h de Paris	The bus will not leave at 5pm from Paris tomorrow
Les cours de cuisine vont commencer la semaine prochaine.	The cooking classes will start next week.	Les cours de cuisine ne vont pas commencer la semaine prochaine.	The cooking classes will not start next week.
Ma mère va acheter des livres et des stylos pour ma petite soeur demain	My mother will buy books and pens for my little sister tomorrow	Ma mère ne va pas acheter des livres et des stylos pour ma petite soeur demain	My mother will not buy books and pens for my little sister tomorrow
Ma famille va parler à sa famille demain au café.	My family will speak to his family tomorrow at the coffee shop.	Ma famille ne va pas parler à sa famille demain au café.	My family will not speak to his family tomorrow at the coffee shop.
Je vais licencier 2 de mes	I will lay off two of my employees	Je ne vais pas licencier mes employés à	I will not lay off my employees

employés à cause de la crise économique.	because of economic crisis.	cause de la crise économique.	because of economic crisis.

Exercise 1

Make the future tense of the following sentences:

1. Tu regardes le match de football de ton équipe de football préférée.
2. L'entreprise embauche 5 nouveaux employés pour le nouveau projet.
3. Les joueurs de cricket jouent très bien le match.
4. Vous soumettez ensemble votre devoir pour le cours de sciences.
5. Charles et Julie démissionnent de leur emploi à Paris en raison du mauvais environnement de travail.
6. Nous lisons les romans du célèbre auteur américain.

Exercise 2

Write down if the following sentences are in Present tense or Future tense:

1. Nous **faisons** notre travail parce que nous voulons obtenir une promotion.
2. Le portefeuille **est** dans sa poche droite du jean avec ses clés.
3. Les livres vont **être** disponibles demain matin à l'accueil de la bibliothèque.
4. Elle va **parler** au directeur à ce sujet.
5. La voiture va **venir** avec plusieurs offres car c'est une saison des festivals.

Exercise 3

Complete the following with the Future tense using the verbs given in the brackets:

1. Je _____ (voir) Paul le week-end prochain après l'école.
2. Tu _____ (demander) à ton professeur ce problème après-demain.
3. Les vacances d'été _____ (commencer) le mois prochain dans notre pays.
4. Nous _____ (acheter) douze gâteaux pour son douzième anniversaire.
5. La pluie _____ (arrêter) dans la soirée selon les bulletins météo.

Exercise 4

1. Write the future negative of the following sentences:
2. Elle danse à l'ouverture de la nouvelle discothèque.
3. Il participe au concours de débat de l'école.
4. Le téléphone dans son sac sonne.
5. Je vais à la banque pour retirer de l'argent.
6. Son père prépare le dîner pour tous ses amis d'école.

Answer Key Chapter 4

Exercise 1

1. Tu vas regarder le match de football de ton équipe de football préférée. (You will watch the soccer game of your favorite soccer team.)
2. L'entreprise va embaucher 5 nouveaux employés pour le nouveau projet. (The company will hire 5 new employees for the new project.)
3. Les joueurs de cricket vont jouer très bien le match. (The cricketers will play the game very well.)
4. Vous allez soumettre ensemble votre devoir pour le cours de sciences. (You will submit together your homework for science class.)
5. Charles et Julie vont démissionner de leur emploi à Paris en raison du mauvais environnement de travail. (Charles and Julie will resign from their jobs in Paris due to the bad working environment.)
6. Nous allons lire les romans du célèbre auteur américain. (We will read the novels of the famous American author.)

Exercise 2

1. Present tense
2. Present tense
3. Future tense
4. Future tense
5. Future tense

Exercise 3

1. Vais voir
2. Vas demander
3. Vont commencer
4. Allons acheter
6. Va arrêter

Exercise 4

1. Elle ne va pas danser à l'ouverture de la nouvelle discothèque.
2. Il ne va pas participer au concours de débat de l'école.
3. Le téléphone dans son sac ne va pas sonner
4. Je ne vais pas aller à la banque pour retirer de l'argent.
5. Son père ne va pas préparer le dîner pour tous ses amis d'école.

Conclusion

Thank you for taking the time to read my guide. I hope you found it useful.

French isn't the easiest language to learn but nor is it the hardest. It is a fun language and, once you have learned the basics, you can easily build up your knowledge. There are several ways you can take your learning further :

- French teaching books
- French courses online, some free, some paid
- Reading French newspapers or books with a translator to hand
- Put post-it notes on items, like the TV, fridge, etc., with the French word and say them aloud
- Watching French TV, starting with English subtitles and then, as you gain more confidence, without subtitles
- Go to France! The locals will love you for trying, and you will always find someone willing to help you improve your language skills.

Whatever you do, practice is key. Don't just learn a few phrases and then forget about it. By the time you come to use them again, you'll have forgotten them, so build a bit of time in every day to speak in French.

French is not just the language of love. It is fun to learn, so go for it – you'll be speaking fluent French inside a month.

Again, Thank You.

As a new travel & language brand with dreams of being big one day, we'd love it and highly appreciate it if you can leave a short review of the book.

We utilize your feedback to keep making this and our future books better so you could have an amazing reading experience!

Free Audiobook

French Fundamentals To Start Conversing Quickly!

SCAN TO ACCESS

Scan QR code above to claim your free audiobook!

— OR —

visit **exploretowin.com/frenchaudio30**

Printed in Great Britain
by Amazon

84566837R00037